Tapestry

Bob Hartman   Susie Poole   Lesley Watmore

Get well soon

When Danny's grandad died,
Danny cried.

And Danny's gran cried too.

A week later, when he went to visit her, she was sorting through his grandad's clothes.

There was the old brown jumper Danny's grandad wore whenever they played football.

There was the faded brown cap he wore the time he showed Danny how to hammer bits of wood into a bird house.

And there were his big brown boots, laces adrift, that Danny had stepped into and stepped onto and skipped beside and scuffed.

But the jumper was empty, and the cap and the brown boots too. And that made Danny sad.

'I really miss Grandad,' said Danny.

'I miss him too,' said Gran. 'But we'll see him again. Jesus promised.'

'How?' asked Danny. 'Where? And when?'

'I'm going away for a while,' she said. 'But when I come back, I'll show you.'

A week went by. Then
two. It felt like forever
to Danny.

And when at last
he went to visit his
gran again, the
clothes were gone.

Instead,
draped over
the table, there
was a picture.

A picture made of cloth.

'It's called a tapestry,' Danny's gran explained. 'I made it while I was away.'

'I like it,' said Danny. 'It's pretty.'

There was the back of a house
that looked a lot like his
gran's. And a garden. And a
shed. And lots of people.

'Look,' said Danny, pointing.
'That's me kicking the ball!'

'It's all of us,' his gran smiled.
'Our whole family.

And your grandad, of course,
building the bird house.

'I put in some other
people too – like
the postman, and
the lollipop lady and
Mrs Martin down
at the sweet
shop.

And Jesus. I thought he
should be there too.
I didn't know what to
make him look
like, but
I thought
he'd be the
one with
the picnic
basket.'

Danny ran his hand gently over the tapestry. It was made of all sorts of cloth – different shapes and shades and sizes.

What caught his attention were the trees. The leaves were shiny and new. But the trunks were woven out of old brown wool.

'That's Grandad's jumper!'
said Danny.

He looked more closely.

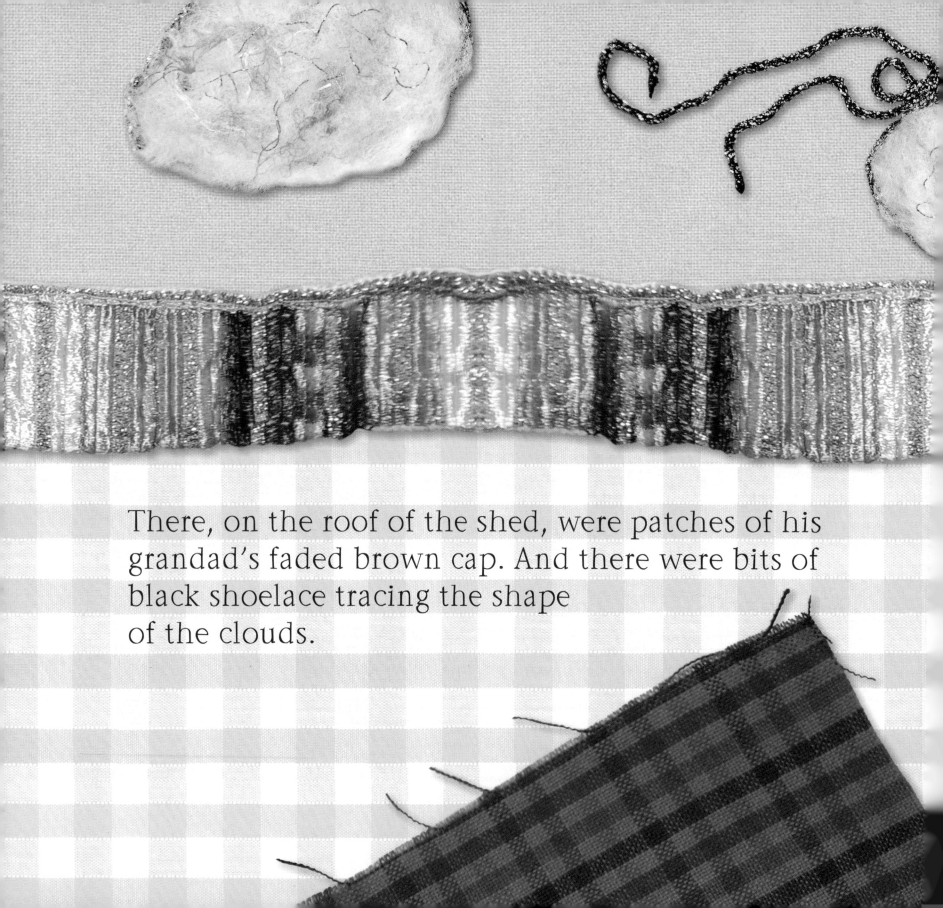

There, on the roof of the shed, were patches of his grandad's faded brown cap. And there were bits of black shoelace tracing the shape of the clouds.

'You asked me when we'd see Grandad again,' said Gran.

'I made the tapestry to help you understand, and as best as I can explain it, it's something like this...

Your grandad is with Jesus – waiting for us in a beautiful place.

But one day...

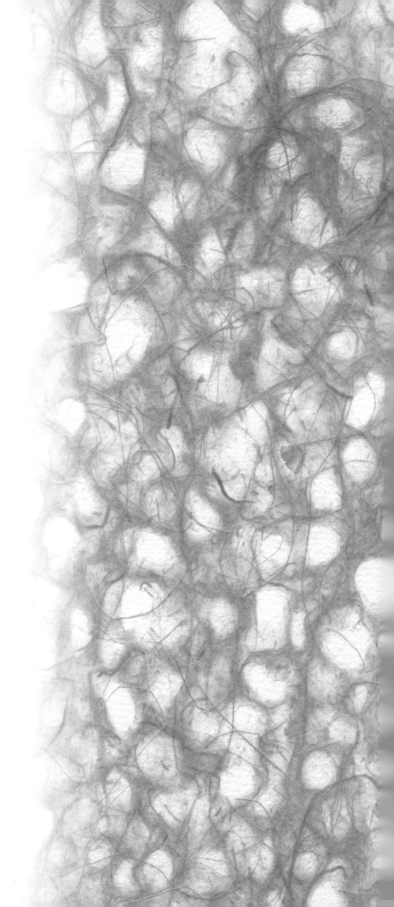

...God is going to make this world of ours all over again,

just like he did for Jesus when he brought him back from the dead.

'He's going to use lots of shiny new things
to make his new world. But I think he's
going to use what's old and familiar as well.

All that we have loved and cherished – the smell
and the shape and the feel of it.

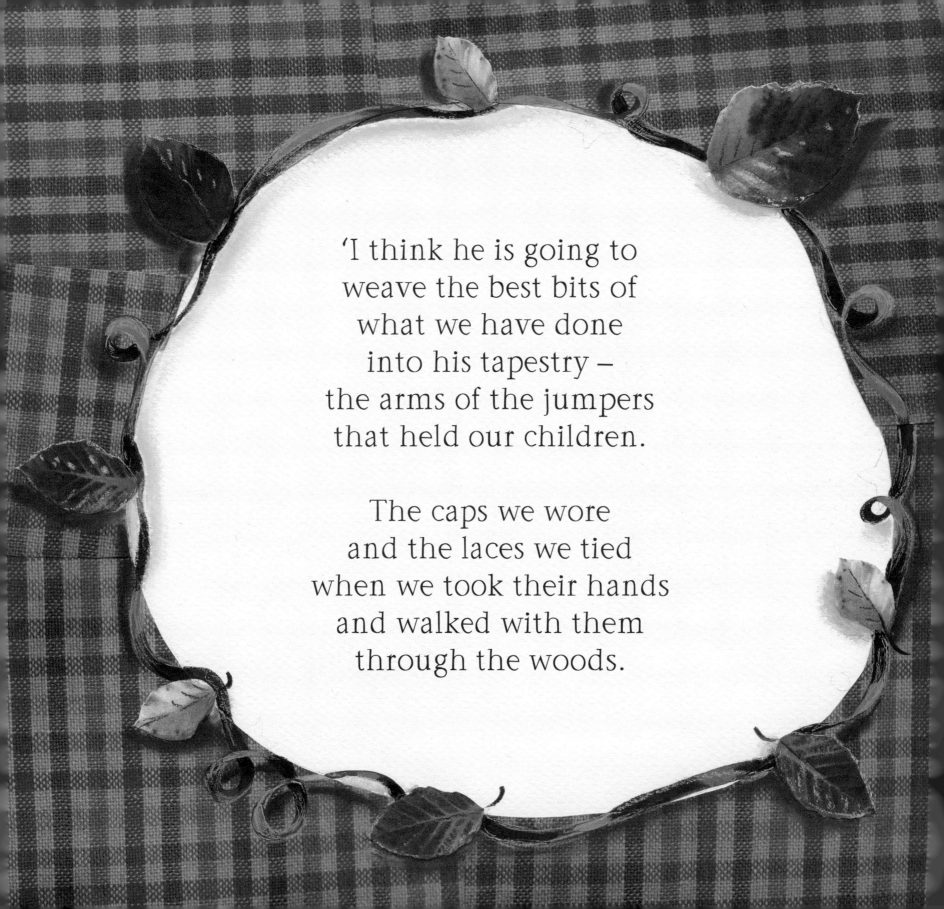

'I think he is going to
weave the best bits of
what we have done
into his tapestry –
the arms of the jumpers
that held our children.

The caps we wore
and the laces we tied
when we took their hands
and walked with them
through the woods.

'You will see your grandad again, Danny.

He will be old and new all at the same time – but you will know him.

And you will kick balls and build bird houses and so much more.

And we will all live in God's new world and share in God's great picnic forever.'

Then she took his hand and she cried.

And Danny cried, too.

But it was a different kind
of crying altogether.

Get well soon